1. Introduction

Over the last two decades, individual hospitals have joined buying arrangements called group purchasing organizations (GPOs), which consolidate the purchasing of member hospitals, effectively turning multiple smaller buyers into larger buyers for the purpose of securing lower prices from vendors. A number of studies have indicated that such organizations have been successful in securing substantial price reductions relative to the prices that could be obtained by individual hospitals.[1]

The case of GPOs is particularly interesting because consolidation under GPOs seems to provide none of the cost savings that might explain the lower prices. A GPO will typically negotiate a set of rates under which member hospitals can purchase from vendors. However, once such rates are set, each hospital arranges for its own delivery schedule and quantities. Thus, many of the economies from coordinated production and/or delivery that might explain lower prices are not present. In addition hospitals are not bound to purchase specific quantities from a given vendor, which seems to rule out quantity commitments that allow for investments of the efficient levels of customer specific assets.[2] It also seems unlikely economies of scale can explain the results since many products are commodity products sold by firms of different size.

The GPO experience seems to be an example of a widely held belief that larger customers command lower prices than smaller customers. This is interesting because it is difficult to show why, in the absence of some form of cost savings, an expected profit maximizing seller would offer lower prices to larger customers. For example, the expected profit maximizing price for one buyer buying 5 units equals the optimal price for five independent buyers each buying one unit if all buyers' valuation distributions are the same.

This paper offers the simple explanation that if an expected utility maximizing seller exhibits risk aversion, then she offers a large customer purchasing a given quantity a lower per unit price than the price she offers a group of smaller identically sized customers purchasing that same quantity. The intuition behind this result is that in a market in which sellers cannot observe buyers' valuations, a customer that is purchasing 5 units is a riskier source of profits than 5 customers with independent valuations each

---

[1] See Scanlon (2002).

purchasing 1 unit. Expected utility maximization suggests that in response to this higher risk, a seller offers the larger customer a lower price. This lower price reduces the expected profit from the large customer, but increases the probability of making the sale. I call this the pure customer size effect.

I identify two other effects. The first is a size of the market effect. I show that an increase in the size of customers that also increases the size of the market can lead to an increase, a decrease or no change at all in the price that customers face. The effect depends on the relative risk aversion of the seller.

The second effect is a customer mix effect. I show that typically when there are two different sized customers, a monopolist will offer the larger customer a lower price than the smaller customer. I also show that when there are small numbers of customers and the utility function of the seller "has a corner" (i.e., is initially steep and then quickly flattens out) it can be optimal for the seller to offer the larger customer a larger price than smaller customers.

It may be argued that since firm owners who can diversify their risk prefer their firms to maximize expected profit, firms should price as if they are risk neutral.[3] However, even if owners could diversify away all risk, the literature provides a number of reasons why a firm would price as if it were risk averse.[4] For example, managers that are responsible for setting prices may be risk averse, and compensation schemes based on the profitability of a product will induce price setting behavior that is affected by the manager's risk aversion.[5] I will also show that firm behavior such as eliminating a product line if it does not meet a firm's target hurdle rate, or offering bonuses to sales people if they reach a given target sales level can also cause managers who maximize their personal expected wealth to offer larger customers lower prices than smaller customers.

The next section reviews the literature on other explanations of quantity discounting and shows why these explanations are not consistent with the type of

---

[2] However, there are often incentive pricing mechanisms that result in hospitals purchasing large portions of their requirements from a single vendor.

[3] Fisher's well known separation theorem states that if owners have perfect access to risk free lending and borrowing, no transactions costs and perfect information, then the composition of their portfolio will be independent of their measure of risk aversion and they will prefer firms to maximize profit.

[4] See section 8 for a discussion of the literature on this topic.

[5] It is well understood that when there are risk averse agents "effective contracts balance the gains from providing incentives against the costs of forcing employees to bear risk." Milgrom and Roberts (1992) pg 208. See also Greenwald and Stiglitz (1990).

quantity discounting examined in this paper. Section 3 presents the benchmark model in which a risk neutral monopolist offers no quantity discounts. Section 4 discusses risk aversion and the pure customer size effect. Sections 5 and 6 examine the confounding effects of changing market size and different sized customers respectively. Extending the intuition to competition is discussed in section 7. Section 8 discusses conditions under which firms behave as if they are risk averse. Concluding remarks are in section 9.

2. Current Literature

The literature has produced a number of explanations for quantity discounts. Cost based explanations argue that cost savings associated with serving large buyers relative to small buyers, result in quantity discounts that reflect the cost. For example, large customers whose order size will result in economies of scale in production or shipping can result in such buyers receiving a lower per unit price.

Demand based explanations do not appeal to such cost savings. Models such as those of Oi (1971) and Maskin and Riley (1989) show that quantity discounts can be used to price discriminate between large and small volume users. While such explanations are undoubtedly valid in many circumstances, they assume that the seller cannot distinguish between high and low volume customers, and uses quantity discounts as a self selection mechanism. Such explanations seem ill suited to explain quantity discounting when sellers can distinguish between large and small volume customers.

Recent work on why larger customers obtain lower prices falls into two categories. First, Snyder (1996, 1998) suggests that when sellers tacitly collude, it is more difficult to prevent a firm from shading price with respect to a large customer than with respect to a small customer. Thus, colluding firms would set lower prices to large customers to reduce the unilateral incentive to shade prices to large customers. While this explanation captures a reasonable notion that sellers will compete more vigorously to serve a large customer than a small customer, a literal interpretation of these results suggest wide spread tacit coordination.[6] My results differ from those of Snyder in that there is no collusion between competing firms. Rather all prices are Nash equilibrium prices of a one shot game.

---

[6] See DeGraba (2003) for a simpler model in which firms compete more vigorously for larger customers but not in which they collude.

4

Second, work by Horn and Wolinsky (1988) Chipty and Snyder (1999) and Chae and Heidhues (1999a, 1999b) look at bargaining between a monopolist and different size buyers. In these models joint surplus between buyers and the seller is increasing, but strictly concave in total output. Each buyer views himself as the marginal buyer, and so bargains over the marginal surplus assuming that all other buyers have completed their bargains. It is assumed that the seller and buyer split the (perceived) surplus, under the Nash bargaining solution. The surplus retained by the seller is interpreted as a payment from the buyer to the seller. Because the surplus function is concave, the average surplus per unit of output is smaller for large buyers than for small buyers. Thus when the surplus is split, the seller receives a lower surplus per unit than he receives from small buyers. This lower surplus is interpreted as a quantity discount.

My results differ from these because in my model neither customers nor sellers treat each transaction as if it is the marginal transaction given all other transactions have been consummated Also, these other works assume that buyers and sellers divide evenly the surplus from a transaction, whereas I determine the division of surplus endogenously.

Recent empirical work by Ellison and Snyder (2001) looks at prices negotiated between large pharmaceutical companies and drug retailers. They compare prices of a drug when it is protected by patents to the prices of the same drug when generic entry occurs. They find that large and small drug retailers pay the same wholesale price when the drug is protected by patent and the larger buyers are able to secure lower per unit prices when there are competing generic drugs.

Their interpretation of the result is that large buyers are not able to obtain quantity discounts from monopolists. My paper suggests a different interpretation. If a monopolist exhibits risk averse behavior, she will offer lower prices to larger buyers if there is unobservable heterogeneity in buyers' valuation of the good. I therefore argue that when a drug is protected by patent buyers are essentially homogeneous with respect to the drug, since their only options are to sell the drug or not sell the drug, and medical plans are likely to pay the same price for the drug across pharmacies. The availability of generics creates heterogeneity among buyers because different buyers will have different willingnesses to substitute the generic for the branded drug. It is this unobservable heterogeneity that causes the drug companies to offer large buyers lower per unit prices.

3. The Benchmark Model

This section presents the benchmark model in which an expected profit maximizing monopolist has no incentive to offer larger buyers a lower price than smaller buyers. There is a monopolist who produces a good at zero marginal cost. She faces a set of customers of mass 1. A given customer values a fixed number of units, each at the same per unit valuation. Each customer's per unit valuation is a random number uniformly distributed on the [0, 1] interval, and is independent of every other customer's valuation.

The seller knows the quantity each customer values, but not his valuation.[7] Given this information she sets a take it or leave it per unit price for each customer. Each customer observes his price, and purchases the number of units he values if his valuation is greater than or equal to the price.[8] The seller's payoff is the profit she realizes from sales.

Observation 1. *If the seller maximizes expected profit, then the optimal price for any customer is $p = \frac{1}{2}$.*

Proof: For any customer that wished to purchase m units, the expected profit from that customer is $(1-p)pm$. The profit maximizing price satisfies $(1-2p)m = 0$. Clearly the optimal price is $\frac{1}{2}$ regardless of the value of m.   *QED*

The intuition is that a customer's maximum expected profit depends only on the distribution of his valuation, and is independent of the number of units he values. Thus, for the expected profit maximizing seller the optimal price is $\frac{1}{2}$ for all customers.

4. The pure customer size effect.

I now alter the benchmark model by assuming the seller is risk averse and maximizes expected utility. I show that this causes her to offer a lower per unit price to larger customers than to smaller customers. In this analysis all customers demand the same number of units. I

---

[7] In the context of GPOs this structure is consistent with the notion that a vendor knows how big each hospital (or group of hospitals) is and therefore how much of a given product each will purchase, but is unsure of how each hospital will value the vendor's product relative to other competing products.

[8] This rather simple "negotiation mechanism" has two important features. First, each customer receives his own price quote. Second, the incomplete information allows for some efficient transactions not to occur. This can be thought of as a proxy for more complex negotiation mechanisms with incomplete information.

compare markets with equal aggregate demand but different numbers of (identically sized) customers. This structure embodies the customer size effect. That is, decreasing the number of customers holding overall demand fixed, thereby increasing customer size, leads to a riskier market. This increased risk creates an incentive for the seller to offer lower prices.

This structure also has important practical implications, because it suggests that increasing customers' size reduces price. This result is interesting because it assumes no market power on the part of customers. In this model customers behave as price takers. This analysis is consistent with the GPO example discussed in the introduction in which hospitals formed buying groups, increasing the size of each customer while holding the overall demand for medical supplies constant.[9]

The monopolist has a concave von Neumann-Morgenstern utility function for profit, $U(\Pi)$, where Π is the profit made from the sales of the good. She chooses prices, p_j to maximize the expected utility from making sales, where j indexes customers. Because Von Neumann-Morgenstern utility functions are unique up to an affine transformation I can normalize U so that $U(0) = 0$.[10]

Proposition 1. *An expected utility maximizing seller with a twice continuously differentiable concave utility function offers a lower price to a single customer of mass 1 than to a continuum of customers with mass 1.*

Proof:

Lemma 1. A risk averse expected utility maximizing seller facing a continuum of customers of mass 1 would set price equal to ½.

Proof. With a continuum of customers whose valuations are i.i.d. uniform $[0, 1]$, the proportion of customers that will purchase at price p' is $1-p'$. Thus, the expected utility function facing the seller is $E(U) = U((1-p)p)$ which reaches its maximum at $p* = $ ½. □

Lemma 2. A risk averse expected utility maximizing seller facing a single customer of mass 1 with valuation distributed uniformly on $[0, 1]$ sets a price less than ½.

---

[9] In the case of GPOs however, not all buying groups increased at the same rate.
[10] Since 0 profit occurs with positive probability, functions such as $\log(\Pi)$ with $U(0)$ undefined are not admissible.

Proof. The seller's objective function is

$$E(U) = (1-p)U(p). \tag{1}$$

The first order condition is

$$\partial E(U)/\partial p = (1-p)U'(p) - U(p). \tag{2}$$

Evaluating (2) at ½ yields $U(½) = \int_0^{1/2} U'(p)\partial p$ which, because U is concave is greater than ½$U'(½)$. Thus, $\partial E(U)/\partial p|_½ < 0$, which implies $p^* < ½$. Figure 1 shows this graphically.

□

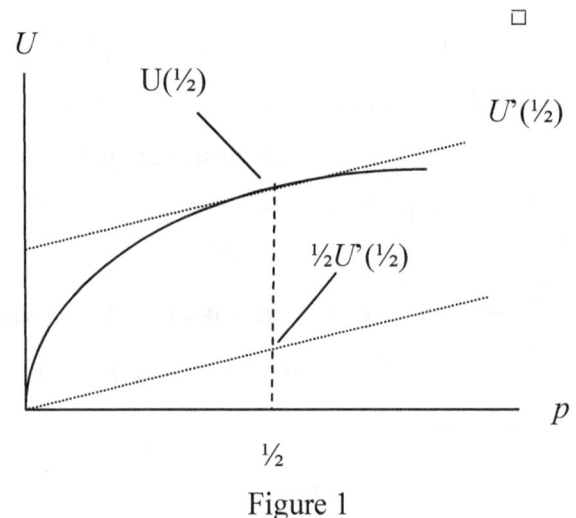

Figure 1

QED

      The intuition behind proposition 1 is that when there is a continuum of customers the demand function is deterministic, so the seller faces no risk. Thus, she sets prices as if she were risk neutral. When facing a single customer, profit is risky, even though the expected profit is the same as when facing a continuum of customers. This risk adds a cost in expected utility terms to the risk averse seller. To reduce this cost by reducing the riskiness of profits, the seller lowers the price.

      With a continuum of customers the seller's expected utility is just U of the profit function arising from a linear demand curve. This profit function has an optimal price of ½. The expected utility with one customer is skewed to the left, so the optimal price is less than ½, as shown in figure 2 below.

8

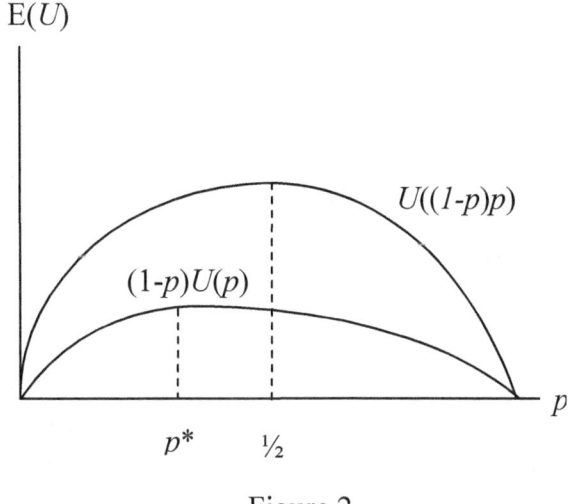

Figure 2

It would seem reasonable to expect that as the number of customers moves from a continuum to 1, the profit function would become more skewed to the left resulting in lower and lower optimal prices as customers become larger (holding market size constant. Proposition 2 compares the price when there are two customers to the price when there is one.

Proposition 2. *An expected utility maximizing seller with a twice continuously differentiable concave utility function offers a lower price to one customer with mass 1 than to two customers each with mass ½.*

Proof: The seller's expected utility when pricing to one customer of mass 1 is

$$E(U) = (1-p)U(p)$$

The first order condition with respect to p is

$$\partial E(U)/\partial p = (1-p)U'(p) - U(p) = 0.$$

Let p^* be the solution to this problem.

The seller's expected utility when facing two customers of mass ½ is

$E(U) = (1-p_1)(1-p_2)U(p_1/2 + p_2/2) + (1-p_1)p_2U(p_1/2) + p_1(1-p_2)U(p_2/2).$

The first order condition is

$$\partial E(U)/\partial p_1 = (1-p_2)[(1-p_1)U'(p_1/2 + p_2/2)(\frac{1}{2}) - U(p_1/2 + p_2/2)] +$$
$$p_2[(1-p_1)U'(p_1/2)(\frac{1}{2}) - U(p_1/2)] + (1-p_2)U(p_2/2).$$

Setting $p_1 = p_2 = p$ yields

$$(1-p)[(1-p)U'(p)(\frac{1}{2}) - U(p)] + p[(1-p)U'(p/2)(\frac{1}{2}) - U(p/2)] + (1-p)U(p/2)$$

and rearranging a bit yields

$$(1-p)[(1-p)U'(p) - U(p_1) - (1-p)U'(p)(\frac{1}{2}) + U(p/2)] + p[(1-p)U'(p/2)(\frac{1}{2}) - U(p/2)]$$

Setting $p = p^*$ and noting $(1-p^*)U'(p^*) - U(p^*) = 0$

$$(1-p^*)[U(p^*/2) - U(p^*)(\frac{1}{2})] + p^*[(1-p^*)U'(p^*/2)(\frac{1}{2}) - U(p^*/2)]$$

The first term in square brackets is always positive for U concave and $p^* < \frac{1}{2}$. In the second square bracket, $(1-p^*)U'(p^*/2)(\frac{1}{2})$ is bounded from below by $(1-p^*)U'(p^*)(\frac{1}{2})$ and therefore $U(p^*)(\frac{1}{2})$. Thus, when the term in the second square bracket is negative, its absolute value is never greater than the term in the first square bracket. Further, since $p^* < \frac{1}{2}$ (proven in proposition 1) the first term is always greater than the second term, implying $\partial E(U)/\partial p_1|_{p^*}$ is positive. This implies the optimal price when there are two customers each of mass $\frac{1}{2}$ is greater than the optimal price when there is one customer of mass 1.   *QED*

These results suggest the pricing behavior of the seller mitigates the risk associated with the uncertainty of profit resulting from customers' unobservable valuations. In this setting a single customer demanding a quantity of 1 represents a riskier source of profit (in the sense of Rothschild and Stiglitz (1970)[11]) than multiple identical customers whose demands sum to 1. The risk averse seller therefore offers a lower price to the single customer to reduce the risk from selling to him.

A slightly different interpretation can be inferred from proposition 2 by making the following observation. Suppose there were two customers of mass ½, but their valuations were perfectly positively correlated. In this case the seller's objective function would be identical to the objective function of the seller facing a single seller of mass 1. Thus, it is not the size of the customer *per se* that creates the incentive for the seller to set the lower price, rather it is the fraction of units for which the reservation prices are perfectly correlated that creates the incentive for the seller to offer the lower price. Thus, reducing the number of customers holding market size constant (effectively increasing the fraction of the units in a market over which each customer can coordinate the reservation price) allows customers to extract lower prices from the seller.

Since these results hold for any concave utility function, they suggests that the fact that risk neutral sellers would set the same price for large and small customers is a "razor's edge" result, and only holds in the cases in which the price setter is exactly risk neutral, or in which there is no effective uncertainty regarding customer valuations. Any thing that would cause a seller not to maximize expected profits, but instead behave as if she were risk averse would result in different prices for different sized customers.

The fact that the price depends on the size of the customers even though all customers are identical is also significant because it suggest the price difference is not a method of extracting different levels of surplus from different size customers (as many quantity discounts do). Rather it is a response to the risk that incomplete information regarding customers' reservation prices imposes on the seller.

To complete the analysis one would like to "fill in" between the two propositions and show that decreasing the number of identical customers from a continuum to one would result in a monotonic decrease in the price. At the moment this general result has eluded the author.

---

[11] Rothschild and Stiglitz show that for a given distribution *f*, an alteration to *g* by a "mean preserving spread" makes all risk averters prefer *f* to *g*.

While I have no general results showing that p falls as n is decreased, I have use Mathematica to calculated optimal prices for utility functions of the form Π^α for $\alpha < 1$ and in these examples p and n are positively related.

5. The market size.

I now consider the effects of allowing the market size to increase by increasing the quantity of each identical customer by the same percentage. This analysis suggests that the price will be affected by how the seller's risk preferences change as the market size changes. I will show constant relative risk aversion causes per unit discounts to remain unchanged as all customers increase in size proportionately,[12] and suggest that decreasing relative risk aversion on the part of the seller may imply an increase in all customers' demand can result in higher prices for all identical customers.

Proposition 3. *Suppose a risk averse expected utility maximizing seller faces n identical customers, each of mass m. Assume the utility function of the seller is Π^α for $0 < \alpha < 1$, where Π is the seller's profit from sales of the good.[13] Then the expected utility maximizing price is independent of m.*

Proof: For any price, p, the expected utility function of the seller is

$$E(U) = \sum_{k=0}^{n} \frac{n!}{(n-k)!k!} (1-p)^k p^{(n-k)} [kmp]^\alpha$$

where k is the number of customers that purchase the good. The first order condition with respect to p is

$$\frac{\partial E(U)}{\partial p} = \sum_{k=0}^{n} \frac{n!}{(n-k)!k!} \{(1-p)^k [p^{(n-k)}\alpha[kmp]^{\alpha-1}km + [kmp]^\alpha(n-k)p^{(n-k-1)}] - p^{(n-k)}[kmp]^\alpha k(1-p)^{k-1}\} = 0.$$

---

[12] Note we cannot use $\log(\Pi)$ because it is undefined at $\Pi = 0$
[13] This proposition also applies to utility functions of the form $-\Pi^\alpha$ for $\alpha > 1$.

Since m appears in each term raised to the α power, it can be eliminated from the expression, proving p is independent of m.   *QED*

The intuition behind this result is that with constant relative risk aversion an increase in the customers' size that also increases the size of the market does not affect the seller's risk assessment. Thus, the discount (relative to the expected profit maximizing price) is independent of the size of the customers.

This result is not limited to a market with identically sized customers.

Corollary 1. For any market with n different sized customers, m_1, m_2 ...m_n, and a seller with a utility function of the form Π^α for $0 < \alpha < 1$, increasing the size of each customer by the same percentage, λ, has no effect on the expected utility maximizing price.

Proof. λ appears in every term of every first order condition raised to the power α and so can be eliminated.   *QED.*

While this result is simple for sellers with constant relative risk aversion, it is not so simple for other functions, though the measure of relative risk aversion is still important. The utility function of a seller facing a single customer of mass m, is

$E(U) = (1-p)U(pm)$.

The first order condition is

$\partial E(U)/\partial p = (1-p)U'(pm)m - U(pm) = 0$

Letting p^* be the solution to this condition, totaling differentiating this with respect to m and rearranging yields that the sign of $\partial p^*/\partial m$ is the sign of:

$$\frac{U''(p^*m)p^*m}{U'(p^*m)} + \frac{1-2p^*}{1-p^*}.$$

This example suggests that an increase in size alone is not sufficient to cause sellers to offer a lower price. Rather it seems that how a change in size affects the seller's risk aversion is an important factor in determining whether an increase in the size of a buyer allows him to command a lower price.

To see how an increase in the size of a customer can result in him being offered a higher price, suppose there is a single customer of mass m, with per unit valuation uniformly distributed on [0, 1]. The seller's utility function is $U(pm) = a + bpm$ for $\Pi \geq \varepsilon$ for ε arbitrarily close to 0 and $U = 0$ for $\Pi < \varepsilon$, a, $b > 0$.[14] The seller's expected utility function for $\Pi > \varepsilon$ is

$$E(U) = (1-p)(a + bpm).$$

Solving the first order condition yields

$$p^* = \frac{1}{2} - \frac{a}{2bm} \quad \text{for } m \geq a/b + 2\varepsilon,$$

$$p^* = \varepsilon/m \quad \text{for } \varepsilon \leq m < a/b + 2\varepsilon,$$

$$\partial p^*/\partial m = a(2bm)^{-2} > 0 \text{ for } m \geq a/b + 2\varepsilon.$$

The intuition behind this result is rather straightforward. The seller's utility consists of 2 pieces, a, which she receives if and only if she makes total sales with value of at least ε, and bpm the utility from the profit from sales in excess of ε. For $m < a/b + 2\varepsilon$, any incremental utility the seller would get from making a sale valued greater than ε/m is outweighed by the loss of expected utility from reducing the probability of making the sale by setting the price above ε/m. Thus it is optimal for the seller when facing such a small customer to set a price equal to ε/m to virtually guarantee a sale is made (even though it generates an arbitrarily small profit) and receive a guaranteed utility of $a + b\varepsilon$.

For $m > a/b + 2\varepsilon$ the seller is willing to trade off some probability of not making a sale for the possibility of increasing profit (and therefore utility) if the sale is made. In fact as m approaches ∞, the optimal price approaches ½ which is the optimal price for a risk neutral seller. This is because as m approaches ∞, a becomes relatively less important, and the utility function approaches bpm the risk neutral utility function. As m increases, for any p, the difference between the seller's expected utility and her utility of the expected profit is a decreasing fraction of the expected utility. Thus, the optimal prices approach the optimal risk neutral price.

6. Customer mix effect

I now consider conditions under which larger customers receive lower prices than smaller customers when the seller serves different sized customers simultaneously. I first show that for "sufficiently small" levels of risk aversion a seller facing two different sized customers always offers a lower price to the larger customer. I then show that for any level of risk aversion, having many small customers and one large customer also results in the large customer receiving a lower price than the small customers.

Finally, I provide numerical analysis using the constant relative risk aversion utility function, $U = \Pi^{\alpha}$, which suggests that for lower to moderate levels of risk aversion larger customers receive lower prices than smaller customers, but for higher, but not too high levels of risk aversion (i.e., for α close to but not too close to 0) there are examples in which one large customer is offered a higher price than one small customers. This result vanishes as the number of customers increases, holding market size fixed.

I assume there are two customers who demand different quantities of the good whenever the price is less than their reservation value. The customers' reservation values are i.i.d. and uniformly distributed on [0, 1].

Proposition 4. For arbitrarily small levels of risk aversion the seller facing two different sized customers sets a lower price to the larger customer.

---

[14] Thus, the seller gets positive utility only if she makes sale valued at ε. Assuming $\varepsilon = 0$ causes the model to degenerate to the case of risk neutrality.

Lemma 3. Let p_L be the price offered to the large customer and p_S be the price offered to the small customer. For any $p_L = p_S \le \frac{1}{2}$, $\partial EU/\partial p_L < \partial EU/\partial p_S$.

Proof: See appendix

Lemma 4. For any concave expected utility function, $E(U)$, if for any $p_L = p_S \le \frac{1}{2}$, $\partial E(U)/\partial p_L$ $< \partial E(U)/\partial p_S$ and if $\partial E(U)/\partial p_i|_{pi = \frac{1}{2}} < 0$ for i $\in \{L, S\}$ then there exist a unique profit maximizing price pair such that $p_L < p_S$.

Proof. For any $p_L' = p_S' < \frac{1}{2}$, the condition $\partial EU/\partial p_L < \partial EU/\partial p_S$ implies there is a higher profit for some any $p_L < p_S < \frac{1}{2}$, and that this profit exceeds the profit for any $p_L > p_S$ within an arbitrarily small neighborhood of $p_L' = p_S'$. Concavity implies that the global optimum is unique, and must occur where $p_L < p_S$. $\partial EU/\partial p_i|_{pi = \frac{1}{2}} < 0$ was established in Lemma 2.

For the risk neutral case of $U = \alpha \Pi$ for $\alpha > 0$, $E(U) = E(\Pi)$ and is therefore strictly concave in p_L and p_S. By continuity any arbitrarily small perturbation in U'' that makes U concave will leave $E(U)$strictly concave   *QED*

Proposition 4 suggests that as a seller moves from being risk neutral to just risk averse the larger customer becomes a riskier revenue source than the smaller customers and so gets a lower price. Proposition 5 provides conditions under which the larger customer always receives a lower price than smaller customers for any level of risk aversion.

Proposition 5. *Suppose a risk averse expected utility maximizing seller faces one customer of mass m and a continuum of customers with mass 1-m, where all customers have per unit valuation i.i.d. uniformly distributed on [0, 1]. The seller sets a lower price for the customer with positive mass than for the continuum of customers.*

Proof: Let p_L be the price offered to the large customer and p_S be the price offered to the small (the continuum of) customers and let q_S be the quantity demanded by the continuum. The continuum generates a demand curve of $q_S = (1-m)(1-p_S)$.

The seller's expected utility function is

$$E(U) = (1-p_L)U(p_L m + p_S q_S) + p_L U(p_S q_S).$$

The first order conditions are

$$\partial E(U)/\partial p_L = (1-p_L)U'(p_L m + p_S q_S)m - U(p_L m + p_S q_S) + U(p_S q_S) = 0,$$

$$\partial E(U)/\partial p_S = \{(1-p_L)U'(p_L m + p_S q_S) + p_L U'(p_S q_S)\}(1-m)(1-2p_S) = 0.$$

The last term of $\partial E(U)/\partial p_S$ implies that $p_S^* = \frac{1}{2}$, regardless of the magnitude of m. Renormalizing U so that $U(p_S q_S) = 0$, allows us to use lemma 2 to show that $p_L^* < \frac{1}{2}$. *QED*

Under the assumptions of proposition 5, the continuum of customers represent a riskless source of profits while the customer with positive mass present the seller with a risky source of profits. Under these conditions the seller sets prices to maximize the expected value of the riskless profit and then chooses the price that maximizes the expected utility from the sales to the customer of mass, m. As proposition 1 suggests, the seller sets a lower price to the risky customer than she does for the continuum of customers that generates the profit that imposes no risk on her.

Despite propositions 4 and 5, a seller will not always offer lower prices to larger customers. Numerical analysis using $U = \Pi^\alpha$ and two different sizes of customers yielded the following results. For α close to 1, the seller offers the larger customer a lower price than the smaller customers. For values of α less than but close to $\frac{1}{2}$ the prices reverse as the seller offers the larger customer a higher price than the smaller customer. For α very close to 0, the prices reverse again and the seller offers the larger customer a lower price. Increasing the number of small customers reduces the level of α at which the seller offers the larger customer a lower price and increasing the number sufficiently eliminates the effect entirely.

This result is based on the fact that for α close to 0 the seller's utility function initially exhibits a large increase in utility for a very small increase in profit above zero, and then exhibits small increases in utility for large increase in profit. It may be helpful to consider again the utility function $U(\Pi) = a - b\Pi$ for $\Pi \geq \varepsilon$ and 0 for $\Pi < \varepsilon$, for ε arbitrarily close to 0.

First consider what happens when $b = 0$. The seller's objective is to maximize the probability of earning at least ε. With two customers of mass $m_1, m_2 > \varepsilon$, the optimal prices are just $p_1 = \varepsilon/m_1$ and $p_2 = \varepsilon/m_2$ so for $m_1 < m_2$, $p_1 > p_2$. Here, since the seller's only concern is earning at least ε, it is optimal for her to set prices so that if either customer makes a purchase, she will earn ε and receive a utility of a.[15] This example corresponds roughly to the case of α arbitrarily close to 0. The larger customer receives the lower price.

Now let b be positive and suppose $m_1 < a/b + 2\varepsilon$ and $m_2 > a/b + 2\varepsilon$. In this case it is optimal to charge customer 1 a price of ε/m_1 virtually ensuring this customer purchases.[16] This allows the seller to behave in an almost risk neutral manner with respect to customer 2. In this case she will set p_2 close to the expected profit maximizing price of ½. This example has the "unusual feature" that all of the risk aversion in the seller's utility function is embodied in receiving a "large amount of utility" a, for making a small sale of ε, and this risk can be virtually eliminated by setting a low price to one of the customers. In this case it is optimal to maximize the probability of making a sale to the smaller customer yielding revenue of ε, and set the price to the larger customer that essentially maximizes expected revenue. This example corresponds to values of α below ½ (but sufficiently greater than 0).

Eliminating this reversal effect can be accomplished by eliminating the specific feature that essentially all of the risk aversion can be eliminated by making a sale to a single small customer. One way to eliminate this effect is to consider values of α close to 1. This mitigates the effect of the "corner" in the utility function and eliminates the ability of the seller to eradicate most of the risk by making a sale to just one customer. A second factor that eliminates this effect is increasing the number of customers. To see why, suppose there are 10 small customers and each is offered a price of ½. The probability that none of these customers purchase is $(½)^{10}$. Thus, even with charging small customers the expected profit maximizing price the seller is virtually assured of making at least one sale valued at ε for ε close enough to zero.

---

[15] A little work is required to show that it is better to set prices so that a sale to only one customer is required to earn a profit of ε rather than setting prices such that both customers must purchase in order to obtain ε.

[16] Recall from the previous section that $m < a/b + 2\varepsilon$ implies the marginal benefit of a price above ε/m is less than the cost of the increased probability of not making a sale.

With this "corner" effect eliminated, the size effect dominates the price setting, and the seller offers the larger customer the lower price.

7. Competing Sellers

In this section I present an example that extends the intuition from proposition 2 to the case of competing firms. In the context of a monopolist it may be difficult to justify the take it or leave it pricing assumption. If a customer refuses to purchase at the announced price one might believe that the seller would offer the buyer a lower price.[17] With competition between sellers a customer that does not purchase from one seller may purchase from the other, so that a seller that does not make an initial sale will have no opportunity to renegotiate.[18] Thus, the purpose of this section is to suggest that the intuition developed in the context of the monopolist is consistent with competition.

There is a Hotelling line of length 1 with seller 0 located at 0 and seller 1 located at 1. Each customer j's location is a random variable uniformly distributed on [0, 1] and independent of the location of other customers. Each customer demands a fixed number of units, and has a per unit travel cost of 1 per unit distance traveled per unit purchased.[19] Thus, for example, a customer located at 1/3 and who values ½ unit has a total travel cost of 1/6 to firm 0 and 1/3 to firm 1. Each customer observes the prices set by the firms and then purchases from the firm at which the total cost is less.

Each seller produces the product at 0 marginal cost, and has a utility function $(\sum_j p_i q_i)^{\alpha}$ for $\alpha \in (0, 1)$. Sellers know the quantity each customer demands, but not his location. Thus, prices can be quantity specific prices, but not location specific.

Given this structure I consider a game in which each sets seller sets a price for each customer simultaneously. Customers' locations are determined, and they make their purchase decisions. Each seller's payoff is her expected utility from the sales she makes.

---

[17] However a seller may want to develop the reputation for not lowering her price once the offer is made. Otherwise all firms would have an incentive to refuse to purchase and wait for a lower price.

[18] One mechanism might be sellers making sealed bids in response to RFPs of buyers, who chooses the lowest bid.

[19] This assumption implies that the total (expected) travel cost remains the same as the number of customers increases. The interpretation of this assumption is that buyers view each unit sold by the firms as differentiated. For example if completing a procedure using a unit of firm 0's product take an additional ½ hour of labor relative to completing it using a unit of firm 1, then the extra cost from using a unit of firm0's product is a ½ hour of labor cost and this would occur for each use of a unit.

Proposition 6: *The equilibrium price when there is a single customer demanding one unit of the good is lower than when there are two customers that each demand ½ unit.*

Proof. When there is a single customer of mass 1, each seller's objective function is

$$E(U_i) = \left[\frac{1}{2} + \frac{p_{-i} - p_i}{2}\right](p_i m)^\alpha.$$

Straightforward analysis shows that the equilibrium price, p^* equals α.

Consider two customers denoted by $j \in \{A, B\}$. Seller i's objective function is

$$E(U_i) = \left[\frac{1}{2} + \frac{p_{-iA} - p_{iA}}{2}\right]\left[\frac{1}{2} + \frac{p_{-iB} - p_{iB}}{2}\right](\tfrac{1}{2}p_{iA} + \tfrac{1}{2}p_{iB}) +$$

$$\left[\frac{1}{2} + \frac{p_{-iA} - p_{iA}}{2}\right]\left[\frac{1}{2} - \frac{p_{-iB} - p_{iB}}{2}\right](\tfrac{1}{2}p_{iA}) + \left[\frac{1}{2} - \frac{p_{-iA} - p_{iA}}{2}\right]\left[\frac{1}{2} + \frac{p_{-iB} - p_{iB}}{2}\right](\tfrac{1}{2}p_{iB})$$

Taking first order conditions with respect to p_{ij} and setting $p_i = p_{-i} = p$ for all j yields:

$$\partial E(U_i)/\partial p_{ij}|_{p_i = p_{-i} = p} = \tfrac{1}{2}[\tfrac{1}{4}\alpha p^{\alpha-1} - \tfrac{1}{2}p^\alpha + \tfrac{1}{4}\alpha(\tfrac{1}{2}\,p)^{\alpha-1} - \tfrac{1}{2}(\tfrac{1}{2}p)^\alpha + \tfrac{1}{2}(\tfrac{1}{2}p)^\alpha].$$

Evaluating this at $p = \alpha$ yields $\partial E(U_i)/\partial p_i = (1/8)[(\tfrac{1}{2})^{\alpha-1} - 1]\alpha^\alpha > 0$ for $\alpha < 1$. Following DeGraba (1993) this implies the Nash equilibrium $p_i^* > \alpha$ for $i \in \{0, 1\}$.[20]   *QED.*

This example is a simple extension of the intuition from the monopoly analysis. A single customer presents a riskier expected profit than do two customers half his size with independently distributed valuations. Competitors respond to the riskier market by offering a lower price.

---

[20] DeGraba (1993) shows that in a game with choice variables that are strategic complements, finding a point, a^+ at which each customer prefers to increase his strategy choice implies there exists an equilibrium in which each customer chooses a value greater than his value at a^+.

8. Why sellers may exhibit risk aversion

The analysis of the previous sections indicates that when risk averse sellers face customers with different demand levels, they have an incentive to offer a lower per unit price to the customers with larger demand. This raises the question of why one should believe that price setters act as if they are risk averse. There are a number of theoretical explanation in the literature for why a firm would behave as if it is risk averse, as well as empirical evidence consistent with firms maximizing expected utility.[21]

One explanation assumes that owners of a firm employ risk averse price setting agents and that the owners are unable to observe perfectly agents' actions. Greenwold and Stiglitz (1990) show that in such situations compensation schemes that are linear in the profits of the firm, or simply giving the agents residual claims on the profits of the firm will make the firm behave as if it is risk averse.

A second explanation is that incomplete information on the part of capital markets may not allow the owner of a firm to fully diversify the risk of the firm through accessing capital markets. Greenwold and Stiglitz (1990) point out that if the owner of a firm has more information about the riskiness of her firm than the market, then she must hold a portion of the risk (i.e., hold more of the firm's equity than in an optimally diversified portfolio) to signal this information to the market. This would cause a risk averse owner to prefer the firm to maximize her expected utility rather than the firm's expected profits. Mas-Colell et. al. (1995) discuss a general equilibrium model in which uncertain demand and risk averse owners result in firms acting as if they are risk averse.

Even if the agent were risk neutral, there are a number of commonly used incentive mechanism that can induce risk-averse like behavior on the part of price setting agents. For example many firms will periodically evaluate projects using hurdle rates. That is, they will continue a project only if its rate of return is above some threshold level. Assuming a manager of such a project would be fired if the project were discontinued, and assuming his other alternative work opportunities offered a lower wage, the expected wage maximizing decision of the price setting manager would be to set prices to maximize the probability that the hurdle rate is met.

---

[21] Empirical studies include Satyanarayan (1999), Applebaum and Ullah (1997), Park and Antonovitz (1992).

To see how this can induce mangers to offer lower prices, I extend the notion of hurdle rates to the benchmark model by assuming h is a profit level needed for a firm to continue a project.[22]

Proposition 7. *When facing a hurdle profit of h, the seller will offer a price to the customer of mass 1 that is less than or equal to the price offered to two customers each of mass ½.*

Proof. When there is just one customer, the probability that the project reaches its hurdle profit of h is maximized when the price per unit is set at h.

Lemma 5. For $h < 2/5$ the expected wage maximizing price when facing two customers is greater than h.

Proof. With two customers the only possible candidate prices are h and $2h$. The former requires that both customers purchase the good for profit to equal h. The latter requires at least one customer to purchase. When the price equals h, the probability that both customers purchase the good is $(1-h)^2$. When the price equals $2h$ the probability at least one customer purchases is $1 - (2h)^2$. $1 - (2h)^2 - (1-h)^2 > 0$ for $h < 2/5$. □

For $h > 2/5$, $1 - (2h)^2 - (1-h)^2 < 0$, so the optimal price is h.
For $h = 2/5$, setting $p = h$ yields the same payoff as setting $p = 2h$. *QED*

The intuition behind this result is that with two customers, setting a price of h means that both customers would have to purchase in order for the seller to earn h. However, for sufficiently low h, it is optimal to set each customer's price at $2h$ so that only one needs to purchase to generate a profit of h. Of course if there were only one customer of mass 1, a price of $2h$ would be too high to reach h, so it would be optimal to lower the price to h to increase (in fact maximize) the probability of earning h without imposing any cost on the price setter since there is no benefit for earning any revenue in excess of h.

---

[22] I need not specify how the optimal hurdle rate is calculated, since the proposition is true for all hurdle profit levels it must be true for the optimal level.

There are other incentive mechanisms and institutional facts that mimic the hurdle rate analysis above. For example a sales person (with discretion over pricing) who receives a bonus only if he reaches a specified sales level would have the same effect as the hurdle rate above. The apparent dependence of stock prices on whether firms meet their quarterly earnings forecast can give managers the incentive to place a lot of weight on meeting earnings forecasts and discount profits above and beyond those forecasts.

9. Conclusion

The question of whether large customers can command lower prices than smaller customers has recently gained attention in the research community. This paper offers a modest explanation of how this may occur. I have shown that increasing the size of a customer, holding the size of the overall market constant increases the riskiness of that customer to a seller. In response to this increase in risk, risk averse sellers will reduce her price to that customer in order to reduce the risk.

Appendix

Proof of Proposition 2.

Show that for $p_1^* < \frac{1}{2}$

$$(1-p_1^*)U^\cdot(p_1^*) - 2U(p_1^*) + p_1^*U^\cdot(p_1^*/2) + 2U(p_1^*/2) - 2p_1^*/(1-p_1^*)U(p_1^*/2) > 0$$

Since $(1-p_1^*)U^\cdot(p_1^*) - U(p_1^*) = 0$ from the first order condition with 1 customer, the problem reduces to showing

$$-U(p_1^*) + p_1^*U^\cdot(p_1^*/2) + 2U(p_1^*/2) - 2p_1^*/(1-p_1^*)U(p_1^*/2) > 0. \qquad (A.1)$$

The proof entails showing that for any twice differentiable utility function, U, condition (A.1) holds for a utility function, V, that goes through the point $(p_1^*, U'(p_1^*))$ and is linear with slope $V' = U'(p_1^*)$ on the interval $[p_1^*/2, p_1^*]$. I then show for any twice differentiable concave function U, V over-estimates $2U(p_1^*/2)$ by less than it underestimates $U'(p/2)$. Thus condition (A.1) also holds for U.

The appropriate condition in terms of the function V is

$$-V(p_1^*) + p_1^*V^\cdot(p_1^*/2) + 2V(p_1^*/2) - 2p_1^*/(1-p_1^*)V(p_1^*/2) \geq 0. \qquad (A.2)$$

Note that because V goes through the point $(p_1^*, U'(p_1^*))$ and has slope $U'(p_1^*)$, the first order condition $(1-p_1^*)V' - V(p_1^*) = 0$ holds.

Lemma 6. The first 3 terms in expression $= V(p_1^*)$
Proof:
$$2V(p_1^*/2) = 2\{V(p_1^*) - (p_1^*/2)V'(p_1^*)\}$$
$$= 2\{(1-p_1^*)V'(p_1^*) - (p_1^*/2)V'(p_1^*)\}$$

Thus $-V(p_1^*) + p_1^*V^\cdot(p_1^*/2) + 2\{(1-p_1^*)V'(p_1^*) - (p_1^*/2)V'(p_1^*)\} = (1-p_1^*)V' = V(p_1^*)$ □

Lemma 7 The last term, $2p_1^*/(1-p_1^*)V(p_1^*/2) \leq V(p_1^*)$
Proof:
$$V(p_1^*/2) = V(p_1^*) - (p_1^*/2)V'(p_1^*)$$
$$= V(p_1^*)(1 - (p_1^*/2)V'(p_1^*)/V(p_1^*))$$
$$= V(p_1^*)(1 - (p_1^*/2)/(1-p_1^*))$$

$$2p_1^*/(1-p_1^*)V(p_1^*/2) = 2p_1^*/(1-p_1^*)V(p_1^*)(1 - (p_1^*/2)/(1-p_1^*))$$

So proving the lemma means showing that for $0 < p_1^* < \frac{1}{2}$

$$2p_1^*/(1-p_1^*)(1 - (p_1^*/2)/(1-p_1^*)) < 1.$$

For $p_1^* = 0$ the expression is zero, for $p_1^* = \frac{1}{2}$ the expression is 1, and the sign of this expression is the sign of $[1 - 2p_1^*/(1-p_1^*)]$ which is positive in the relevant range. □

Lemma 8. If condition (A.2) holds then condition (A.1) holds.
Proof:
It suffices to show that $2V(p_1*/2)$ is less of an overestimate of $2U(p_1*/2)$ than p_1*V' is an underestimate of $p_1*U'(p_1*/2)$, because this would mean the first 3 terms of (A.1) are greater than their counterparts in (A.2) and the last term in (A.1) is more negative than its counterpart in (A.2). This is a direct result of the concavity of U. The difference between the $V(p_1*/2)$ and $U(p_1*/2)$ is simply $(p_1*/2)(S' - V')$ where S' is the slope of the line between $U(p_1*/2)$ and $U(p_1*)$. Thus twice this difference is $(p_1*)(S' - V')$. The difference between $(p_1*)(V')$ and $p_1*U'(p_1*/2)$ is $p_1*(U'(p_1*/2) - V')$. $U'(p_1*/2) > S'$ by the concavity of U. □

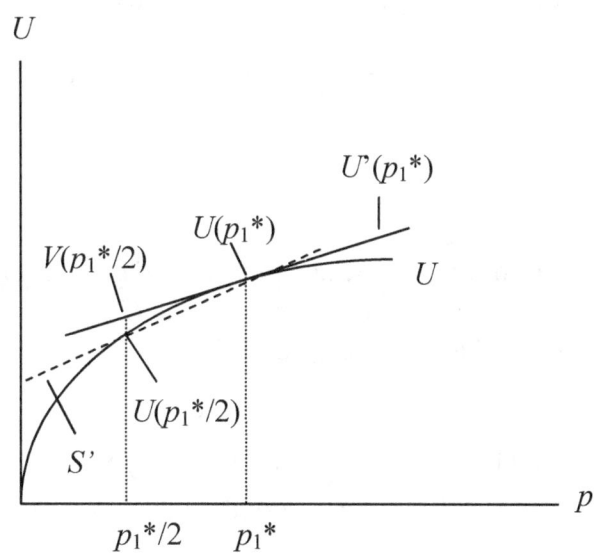

Proof of Proposition 4 – Lemma 3
$\mathrm{E}(U) = (1-p_L)(1-p_S)U(p_LL + p_SS) + (1-p_L)p_SU(p_LL) + p_L(1-p_S)U(p_SS)$

$\partial\mathrm{E}(U)/\partial p_L = (1-p_S)\{(1-p_L)U'(p_LL + p_SS)L - U(p_LL + p_SS)\} + $
$\qquad\qquad\qquad\qquad p_S\{(1-p_L)U'(p_LL)L - U(p_LL)\} + (1-p_S)U(p_SS)$
$\partial\mathrm{E}(U)/\partial p_S = (1-p_L)\{(1-p_S)U'(p_LL + p_SS)S - U(p_LL + p_SS)\} + $
$\qquad\qquad\qquad\qquad p_L\{(1-p_S)U'(p_SS)S - U(p_SS)\} + (1-p_L)U(p_LL)$

Set $p_S = p_L$

$\partial\mathrm{E}(U)/\partial p_L = (1-p)U'(pL + pS)L - U(pL + pS) + p/(1-p)\{(1-p)U'(pL)L - U(pL)\} + U(pS)$
$\partial\mathrm{E}(U)/\partial p_S = (1-p)U'(pL + pS)S - U(pL + pS) + p/(1-p)\{(1-p)U'(pS)S - U(pS)\} + U(pL)$

$\partial\mathrm{E}(U)/\partial p_L = (1-p)U'(pL + pS)L + p[U'(pL)]L - p/(1-p)U(pL) + U(pS) - U(pL + pS)$
$\partial\mathrm{E}(U)/\partial p_S = (1-p)U'(pL + pS)S + p[U'(pS)]S - p/(1-p)U(pS) + U(pL) - U(pL + pS)$

25

understate $U(pL)$ as $U(pS)+U'(pL)(L\text{-}S)$ in $\partial E(U)/\partial p_L$ in $\partial E(U)/\partial p_S$ to overstate $\partial E(U)/\partial p_L$ and understate $\partial E(U)/\partial p_S$.

$\partial E(U)/\partial p_L = (1\text{-}p)U'(pL + pS)L + p[U'(pL)]L - p/(1\text{-}p)[U(pS)+U'(pL)(L\text{-}S)]+ U(pS) - U(pL + pS)$

$\partial E(U)/\partial p_S = (1\text{-}p)U'(pL + pS)S + p[U'(pS)]S - p/(1\text{-}p)U(pS) + U(pS)+U'(pL)(L\text{-}S) - U(pL + pS)$

subtracting $\partial E(U)/\partial p_S$ from $\partial E(U)/\partial p_L$ yields

$\Delta = (1\text{-}p)U'(pL+pS)(L\text{-}S) + p[U'(pL)L\text{-} U'(pS)S] - p/(1\text{-}p)[U'(pL)(L\text{-}S)]\text{-}U'(pL)(L\text{-}S)$

writing $-U'(pL)(L\text{-}S)$ as $-[(1\text{-}p) - p]U'(pL)(L\text{-}S)$ and rearranging yields

$\Delta = (1\text{-}p)[U'(pL+pS) \text{-}U'(pL)](L\text{-}S) + p[U'(pL)S\text{-} U'(pS)S] - p/(1\text{-}p)[U'(pL)(L\text{-}S)]$

$\Delta < 0$ because concavity of U implies $(1\text{-}p)U'(pL + pS) < U'(pL) < U'(pS)$ $\qquad\qquad$ □

Proof of Proposition 5

For α close to 1 I need to show that, for the p' at which $p_L = p_S = p'$ $\partial E(U)/\partial p_L|_{p'} = 0$, $\partial E(U)/\partial p_S|_{p'} > 0$, and similarly for the p'' at which $p_L = p_S = p''$ $\partial E(U)/\partial p_S|_{p''} = 0$, $\partial E(U)/\partial p_L|_{p''} < 0$. Further I must show that $\partial p^*{}_S/\partial p^*{}_L$ and $\partial p^*{}_L/\partial p^*{}_S < 1$ for values of p_L and p_S between 0 and ½.

$\partial E/\partial p_L = (1\text{-}p)[(1\text{-}p)\alpha p^{\alpha\text{-}1}L - p^{\alpha}] + p[(1\text{-}p)\alpha(pL)^{\alpha\text{-}1}L - (pL)^{\alpha}]+ (1\text{-}p)(pS)^{\alpha} = 0$

$\partial E/\partial p_S = (1\text{-}p)[(1\text{-}p)\alpha p^{\alpha\text{-}1}S - p^{\alpha}] + p[(1\text{-}p)\alpha(pS)^{\alpha\text{-}1}S - (pS)^{\alpha}]+ (1\text{-}p)(pL)^{\alpha}$

$\partial E/\partial p_L = (1\text{-}p)\alpha p^{\alpha\text{-}1}L - p^{\alpha} + \alpha(pL)^{\alpha} - p(pL)^{\alpha}/ (1\text{-}p)]+ pS^{\alpha} = 0$

References

Applebaum, Elie, and Aman Ullah, (1997) "Estimation of Moments and Production Decisions Under Uncertainty," *Review of Economics and Statistics*, November 79, 631-37.

Chae, Suchan and Paul Heidhues (1999a) "Bargaining Power of a Coalition in Parallel Bargaining; Advantages of Multiple Cable System Operators," mimeo.

Chae, Suchan and Paul Heidhues (1999b) "The Effects of Downstream Distributor Chains on Upstream Producer Entry: A Bargaining Perspective." mimeo.

Chipty, Tasneem (1995) "Horizontal Integration for Bargaining Power: Evidence from the Cable Television Industry," Journal *of Economics and Management Strategy* Vol. 4, pp 375-397.

Chipty, Tasneem and Christopher M. Snyder (1999) "The Role of Firm Size in Bilateral Bargaining: A Study of the Cable Television Industry," *Review of Economics and Statistics* Vol. 81 pp 326-340.

DeGraba, Patrick (1993) "Characterizing solutions of supermodular games; intuitive comparative statics and unique equilibria," Economic Theory 5, 181-188.

DeGraba, Patrick, (2003) "Volume Discounts, Loss Leaders, and Competition for More Profitable Customers," Working Paper Federal Trade Commission.

Ellison, Sara, and Christopher Snyder, (2001) "Countervailing Power in Wholesale Pharmaceuticals," MIT Department of Economics Working Paper 01-27 July.

Greenwald. Bruce and Joseph Stiglitz (1990) "Asymmetric Information and the New Theory of the Firm: Financial Constraints and Risk Behavior," *American Economic Review*, May, 80 160-165.

Horn, Henrick and Asher Wolinsky (1988) "Bilateral Monopolies and the Incentive to Merge," *Rand Journal of Economics* Vol. 19 pp 408 - 419.

Maskin, Eric and John Riley (1984) "Optimal auctions with risk-averse buyers," *Econometrica,* 52(6):1473-1518, 18.

Maskin, Eric and John Riley (1989) "Optimal multi-unit auctions." In F. Hahn, editor, *The Economics of Missing Markets, Information, and Games.* Oxford University Press, Clarendon Press, 13.

Mas-Colell, Andreau, Michael D. Whinston, and Jerry Green (1995) *Microeconomic Theory*, New York: Oxford University Press.

Milgrom Paul, and John Roberts (1992) *Economics Organization, and Management*, Prentice Hall, Englewood Cliffs, New Jersey.

Oi, Walter, (1971) "A Disneyland dilemma: Two part Tariffs for a Mickey Mouse Monopoly," *Quarterly Journal of Economics* 85, pg77-96.

Park Timothy and Frances Antonovitz, (1992) "Econometric Tests of Firms Decision Making Under Uncertainty: Optimal Output and Hedging Decisions," *Southern Economic Journal* 58, 593-609.

Rothschild, Michael and Joseph Stiglitz (1970) "Increasing Risk: 1. A Definition" *Journal of Economic Theory*, 2, 225-243.

Satyanarayan, Sudhakar, (1999) "Econometric Tests of Firm Decision Making Under Dual Sources of Uncertainty," *Journal of Economics and Business*, 51, 315-25.

Scanlon, William J., (2002) "Group Purchasing Organizations Pilot Study Suggests Large Buying Groups Do Not Always Offer Hospitals Lower Prices," Government Accounting Office, April 30, 2002, GAO-02-690T.

Snyder, Christopher. M. (1996) "A Dynamic Theory of Countervailing Power," *Rand Journal of Economics* Vol. 27 pp 747-769.

Snyder, Christopher. M. (1998) "Why Do Larger Buyers Pay Lower Prices," *Economics Letters* Vol. 58 pp 205-209.